DECISIVE BATTLES

Tim Cooke

Gareth Stevens
Publishing

Please visit our website, www.garethstevens.com. For a free color catalog of all our high-quality books, call toll free 1-800-542-2595 or fax 1-877-542-2596.

Library of Congress Cataloging-in-Publication Data
Cooke, Tim.
Decisive battles / Tim Cooke.
    p. cm. — (The American Civil War: the right answer)
Includes index.
ISBN 978-1-4339-7540-0 (pbk.)
ISBN 978-1-4339-7541-7 (6-pack)
ISBN 978-1-4339-7539-4 (library binding)
1. United States—History—Civil War, 1861-1865—Campaigns. I. Title.
E470.1.C75 2012
973.7'3—dc23

                                         2012004972

Published in 2013 by
Gareth Stevens Publishing
111 East 14th Street, Suite 349
New York, NY 10003

© 2013 Brown Bear Books Ltd.

For Brown Bear Books Ltd:
Editorial Director: Lindsey Lowe
Managing Editor: Tim Cooke
Children's Publisher: Anne O'Daly
Art Director: Jeni Child
Designer: Karen Perry
Picture Manager: Sophie Mortimer
Production Director: Alastair Gourlay

Picture Credits:
Front Cover: Library of Congress

Interior all Library of Congress except, National Archives: 35; Robert Hunt Library: 29.

All Artworks © Brown Bear Books Ltd.

Manufactured in the United States of America
1 2 3 4 5 6 7 8 9   12 11 10

CPSIA compliance information: Batch #BRS12GS: For further information contact Gareth Stevens, New York, New York at 1-800-542-2595.

Contents

Introduction

The Civil War (1861–1865) was made up of a series of set battles punctuated by smaller fights. It was the bloodiest conflict in history until that time: more than 600,000 men died on the battlefields.

The Civil War that began in 1861 saw a whole generation of young men called into military service. Both the North and the South began the conflict with great enthusiasm. Volunteers flocked to enlist. It soon became apparent that the war would be long and bloody, however. Casualties were far higher than anyone had expected. Ultimately, both sides turned to conscription to make sure that they always had enough men available to fight.

The generals who commanded the fighting were of varied quality. Many had been trained together before the war. Former colleagues and friends from the United States Army now found themselves facing one another in battle.

As the war went on, a new generation of generals came to prominence. They included some of the greatest military commanders in American history: men such as Ulysses S. Grant and William T. Sherman for the Union, and Robert E. Lee and Thomas "Stonewall" Jackson for the Confederacy.

About this book

This book describes the main battles that shaped the course of the war. The articles are arranged in chronological order to make it easier to see how each battle was related to those that came before and after it. Boxes in the margins help you get more out of your reading. **Comment** boxes highlight specific information and explain its importance. **Ask Yourself** boxes suggest questions for you to consider. There are no right or wrong answers; the questions are meant to help you think about the subject. Other boxes explain difficult words or ideas. The book finishes with a glossary and a list of resources for further information. There is also an index that you can use to find facts fast.

Confederates face a Union attack at Missionary Ridge, near Chattanooga, Tennessee, in November 1863.

Bull Run (Manassas)

The First Battle of Bull Run, also known as the First Battle of Manassas, was the first large battle of the war. The Union and Confederate armies met on July 21, 1861, in northern Virginia.

◯ *A Zouave in a fez leads a Confederate charge against the Union lines.*

The war had only begun a couple of months earlier. Both sides thought they were stronger than the other. And both thought the war would be over very quickly. The First Battle of Bull Run showed that they were both wrong.

In the North, President Abraham Lincoln had gathered a large army of volunteers. By early summer, the population wanted him to send troops to attack the Confederate capital at Richmond, Virginia. General Irvin McDowell led the main Union force of 35,000 men. He protested that they were not ready to fight. But Lincoln ordered McDowell to leave for Richmond.

The armies meet

In McDowell's way was another inexperienced force. The main Confederate army of 20,000 men was led by Pierre G. T. Beauregard. They were located north of Manassas Junction, only 30 miles (48 km) from Washington, D.C. Manassas was a Confederate supply depot. Beauregard was reinforced by 12,000 troops commanded by General Joseph E. Johnston. They were moved rapidly to the battlefield by railroad.

McDowell's first chance to attack came on July 16. Just as he had warned, his troops were not well enough trained. The enemy troops escaped. On July 18, there was another skirmish that lasted most of the afternoon. Again, the Confederates repelled the Union forces.

ASK YOURSELF

Should Lincoln have put pressure on McDowell after his general had said that his troops were not ready?

Main battle

Both armies spent the next days regrouping and carrying out reconnaisance. Both leaders chose the same battle plan for July 21: they both planned to attack the enemy's left flank.

On the 21st, McDowell struck first. An alert Confederate signal officer spotted the movement.

↩ *Union troops of the Sixty-Ninth New York Regiment charge enemy artillery positions.*

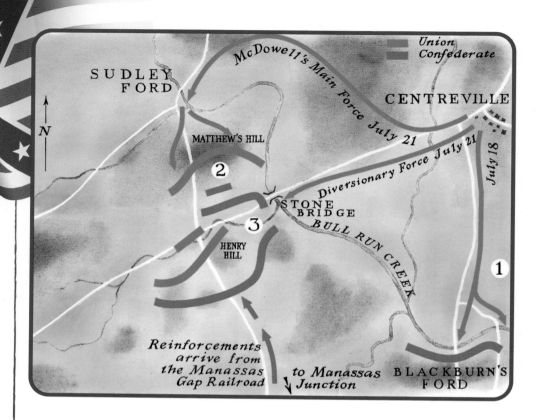

Union
Confederate

SUDLEY FORD

McDowell's Main Force July 21

CENTREVILLE

N

MATTHEW'S HILL

Diversionary Force July 21

July 18

STONE BRIDGE

BULL RUN CREEK

HENRY HILL

Reinforcements arrive from the Manassas Gap Railroad

to Manassas Junction

BLACKBURN'S FORD

🎧 *This map shows the different movements of the two armies over the course of the four-day battle.*

Using signal flags for the first time in the war, he gave the Confederates time to form their defenses. The troops clashed on Matthew's Hill in a bloody struggle. For many of the troops, it was their first, terrifying experience of conflict.

Confederate counterattack

McDowell's army was larger. By late morning, it had pushed the Confederates back to Henry Hill. They were almost beaten, but reinforcements arrived in the nick of time. Led by Thomas Jackson, they counterattacked on the slopes of Henry Hill. Jackson's defense earned him his famous nickname of "Stonewall." Other

Confederate brigades attacked, and McDowell's exhausted forces were pushed back. By evening, Union troops were heading toward Washington. The retreat descended into mayhem as troops became mixed up with the wagons of civilian spectators. When the Confederates shelled the road, the disorderly retreat became a panic.

There were few casualties compared to later battles of the war: 1,900 Confederate casualties and 2,800 from the Union. But First Bull Run showed the commanders that their men needed better training. It also proved the value of railroads for moving troops. And it destroyed any ideas that the war would soon be over.

> Union civilians had traveled out from Washington, hoping to see an easy Union victory.

> **ASK YOURSELF**
>
> How might the public on both sides have reacted when they realized that the war would be a long one?

THE RIGHT ANSWER

?

How did the First Battle of Bull Run set the pattern for other battles in the Civil War?

The officers on both sides had trained at the same military institutions. Many were former colleagues, and they often used similar tactics. At First Bull Run, they both set out to attack the enemy's left flank. The battle showed the importance of being able to maneuver troops quickly into position on the battlefield. It also showed the advantage of moving men over long distances by railroad. It introduced a new hero for the Confederacy—"Stonewall" Jackson. At the same time, it showed the weakness of some generals who were appointed because of their political views.

Hampton Roads

The Battle of Hampton Roads took place off the coast of Virginia on March 8–9, 1862. It was an important event in naval history because it was the first clash of armored ships, or "ironclads."

COMMENT

Ironclads were far tougher than the wooden warships that were used before the war.

At the start of the Civil War, the Union had taken a highly significant step. It had set up a naval blockade of the Southern coastline. It wanted to stop Southern imports and exports. In particular, it wanted to stop the shipment of cotton to the international market. To break the blockade, the Confederacy developed a new kind of ship that had never been seen in warfare. Ironclads were ships covered with iron armor.

The Confederates converted the *Merrimack*, a partly destroyed Union ship they had captured. They covered its hull with 4-inch-thick (10 cm thick)

➲ *The two ironclads fought at close quarters for almost four hours, but neither could get the upper hand.*

The crew of the Union ironclad Monitor at Hampton Roads in an 1862 photograph that has been colored by hand.

armor plating made from iron. They also attached an iron ram to its bow. The Confederates renamed the ship the CSS *Virginia*.

During its first trial cruise from Norfolk, Virginia, the ship steamed into Hampton Roads on March 8, 1862. Its commanding officer, Franklin Buchanan, decided to see what his new vessel was capable of. The CSS *Virginia* attacked Union ships blockading Chesapeake Bay.

In a short space of time, the *Virginia* destroyed two large Union warships, the USS *Cumberland* and USS *Congress*, and damaged the USS *Minnesota*. In only a few hours, the ironclad had changed the course of naval warfare. It had shown that the wooden, sail-powered ships that had gone before were now out of date.

Hampton Roads was the worst defeat the United States Navy would suffer until the bombing of Pearl Harbor in 1941, during World War II.

The ironclads do battle

Next morning, the victorious CSS *Virginia* returned to Hampton Roads to continue the battle. Much to the surprise of its crew, an enemy ironclad, the USS *Monitor*, was waiting for it.

The *Monitor* was smaller than the *Virginia*, but it had a revolving gun turret and a shallower draft, and it could move faster. These features meant the *Monitor* could outmaneuver the *Virginia* in the battle that followed.

The two ships attacked each other at close range for almost four hours. Their guns blazed throughout the afternoon. As night fell, they reached a stalemate. The *Virginia* withdrew into the James River. Over the two days, it had been hit 97 times, and the *Monitor* 21 times. Because of

The U.S. Congress gave permission for ironclads on August 3, 1861, and a commission to oversee the designs was formed.

↻ *A wooden warship burns while* Monitor *and* Virginia *clash in Hampton Roads.*

their armor, neither ship was badly damaged. But the strategic victory belonged to the Union, which had kept up its blockade.

Significance of the battle

Although it was a minor battle, the clash at Hampton Roads signaled a change in warfare. Both sides sped up their naval building programs. The Union could produce more ironclads than the Confederacy, however, so kept its superiority at sea. As for the *Virginia*, it was sunk by its crew four months later to stop it falling into enemy hands after Union troops captured the Norfolk shipyard where it was based.

> The revolving turret inspired later warships and became a standard feature.

> **ASK YOURSELF**
>
> Why might the Union have found it easier to produce ironclads than the Confederates?

THE RIGHT ANSWER

?

What was the significance of the Battle of Hampton Roads to the outcome of the war?

The introduction of ironclads into naval warfare changed the nature of the war. Both sides now had to compete with more modern technology. For the Union, this was not a problem. Its industrial production was almost nine times greater than that of the Confederacy. By contrast, the Confederacy was an agriculture-based economy with little use for factories or iron. The South had traditionally relied on European or Northern ships to transport its cotton across the globe. It was slow to set up a Southern ship-building industry, and by the time it did, it was too late.

Shiloh

Shiloh was one of the bloodiest battles of the war. It was fought on the Tennessee River on April 6–7, 1862, by Ulysses S. Grant's Union forces and the Confederate army of General Albert S. Johnston.

🎧 *Union troops advance toward the fighting in this print made at the time of the battle.*

COMMENT

The weather often had an influence on the progress of the war, particularly if heavy rain turned the roads to mud.

In February 1862, General Ulysses S. Grant had captured Forts Henry and Donelson. That gave the Union control over the Tennessee and the Cumberland Rivers. Johnston was forced to retreat, leaving the way open for Union forces to move south.

By March, two Union armies were ready to enter Mississippi. Grant led his 30,000 men to Pittsburg Landing, 25 miles (40 km) north of Corinth, Mississippi. Don Carlos Buell's army of 50,000 men prepared to join him from Nashville.

Johnston decided to try to defeat Grant before Buell arrived. That would win back Confederate control in Tennessee and Mississippi. In early April, Johnston and 45,000 men headed for Pittsburg Landing to make a surprise attack. Bad weather and disorganization slowed them down, however, and they arrived later than planned.

The rebel yell

Johnston still had the advantage. Grant had not posted lookouts, so the Union soldiers had no idea there was a Southern army nearby. Just after 5:00 A.M. on April 6, thousands of men in gray charged from the woods, screaming the rebel yell.

The Confederates first attacked the Union right and center. They pushed the Union right back toward the river at Pittsburg. But the center and left of the Union line held their ground for almost five hours. At the heart of the fighting, there were so many buzzing bullets that the position was called the "Hornets' Nest." It saw some of the fiercest hand-to-hand fighting in the whole war.

By early afternoon, Johnston became worried about his right flank. He called up his reserves. Shortly afterward, however, he was shot and bled to death. He was replaced by his junior officer, General Pierre G. T. Beauregard.

The rebel yell was a battle cry used by Confederate soldiers. As they charged, they yelled to scare their Union opponents and to boost their morale.

ASK YOURSELF

How many bullets must have been fired for the site of fighting to have been nicknamed the "Hornets' Nest?"

◑ The two sides clash at close quarters in the Hornets' Nest, scene of some of the most intense fighting in the whole war.

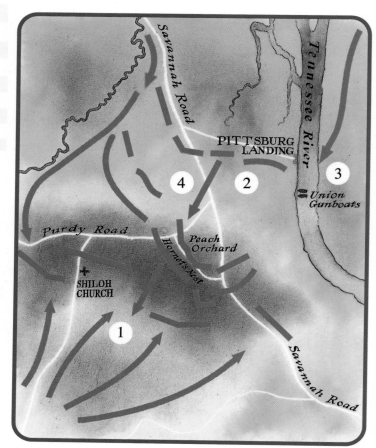

⮑ **This map shows the positions of both sides from the Confederate attack (red) to the Union counterattack (blue).**

Confederate troops had succeeded in pushing back Union troops to the river by nightfall. This gave them the advantage.

Union collapse

As his men desperately held their lines, Grant organized Union reinforcements. His army was now on the very brink of defeat. Union soldiers flooded back to the riverbank at Pittsburg Landing. The defense in the Hornets' Nest ended in surrender at about 5:30 P.M. If Beauregard had pressed on with the attack, the Confederates might have won the battle. But they were worn out after 14 hours of fighting. At 7:00 P.M., they stopped for the night to rest.

The next day

Overnight, Grant was able to organize his troops and reinforcements. He launched a counterattack early on April 7. The Confederates lost all the ground they had won the day before. They began to fall back— and ended up retreating all the way to Corinth.

Shiloh was one of the bloodiest battles of the whole war. The Confederates had suffered 10,700 casualties for no gain. The North had lost 13,000 casualties and only just avoided defeat.

This view shows part of the battle from a Confederate artillery position.

THE RIGHT ANSWER

?

Could the Confederates have avoided defeat at Shiloh and pushed the Union back?

The Confederates had the upper hand at the end of the first day. They lost the battle because their troops were too tired to go on fighting. They therefore failed to secure the victory before Buell's reinforcements could arrive. The next day, April 7, they faced a much larger enemy force. The Union now had 45,000 men, while the total Confederate force was only 20,000. Johnston's death was also a severe blow to the Confederate cause. With 8,500 casualties and many desertions on the first day, Beauregard probably felt he had no option other than to withdraw when he did.

Peninsular Campaign

In March 1862, General George B. McClellan led Union forces in a campaign toward the Confederate capital of Richmond, Virginia. He planned to attack from the coast across the Virginia Peninsula.

McClellan came up with the plan to take advantage of the Union navy's control of the coast. He could move his army into position by boat. President Abraham Lincoln was reluctant to allow the plan. He was worried that McClellan would leave Washington, D.C., unprotected from a Confederate advance.

McClellan said he would leave enough troops to defend the capital, but Lincoln had his own ideas. He ordered a whole corps from McClellan's command to stay in northern Virginia. The breakdown of trust between the two men would affect the outcome of the campaign.

⟳ *Union artillery in action at Malvern Hill on July 1, 1862, the last battle of the Peninsular Campaign.*

McClellan departs

By April 1, 1862, McClellan had moved 60,000 men and 100 guns to Fort Monroe, on the Virginia coast. Another 40,000 men would follow. In response, the Confederate

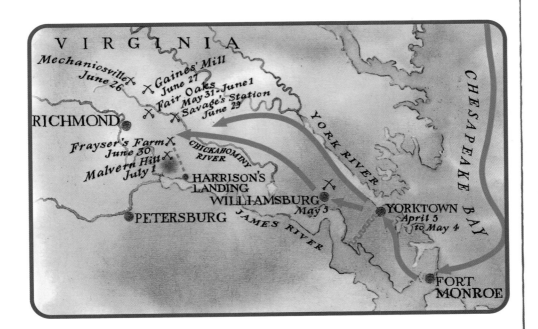

Map labels:
VIRGINIA
Mechaniosville June 26
Gaines' Mill June 27
Fair Oaks May 31-June 1
Savage's Station June 29
RICHMOND
Frayser's Farm June 30
Malvern Hill July 1
CHICKAHOMINY RIVER
HARRISON'S LANDING
WILLIAMSBURG May 3
PETERSBURG
JAMES RIVER
YORK RIVER
YORKTOWN April 5 to May 4
FORT MONROE
CHESAPEAKE BAY

general John B. Magruder built defensive lines between the York and the James Rivers. He also tricked McClellan into believing that his tiny force was much larger than it was. McClellan thought he faced at least 100,000 Confederates.

Instead of advancing, McClellan laid siege to Yorktown. Lincoln urged him to advance, but McClellan ignored him. The halt gave the Confederates time to reinforce Magruder with General Joseph E. Johnston's army. The Confederates now had 75,000 troops on the south bank of the Chickahominy River.

The armies clash

By the end of May, the two armies faced one another around the villages of Fair Oaks and Seven Pines. McClellan split his army into two,

This map shows the route of McClellan's Army of the Potomac as it advanced toward the Confederate capital.

McClellan's decision to lay siege to Yorktown instead of attacking was a fatal error. It allowed the Confederates time to send reinforcements.

with 60,000 men on the north side of the river and 31,500 on the south side.

On May 31, Johnston attacked. The attack was poorly executed, and the Confederates suffered 6,150 casualties. Johnston himself was badly injured. General Robert E. Lee took command and ordered an immediate withdrawal.

Lee in command

For two weeks, both sides consolidated their positions in pouring rain. When Lee learned that McClellan had left only one corps on the north bank of the river near Mechanicsville, Lee decided to attack. The Battle of Mechanicsville on

↻ *This map shows the Union retreat (red) and the battles the army fought on its way to safety.*

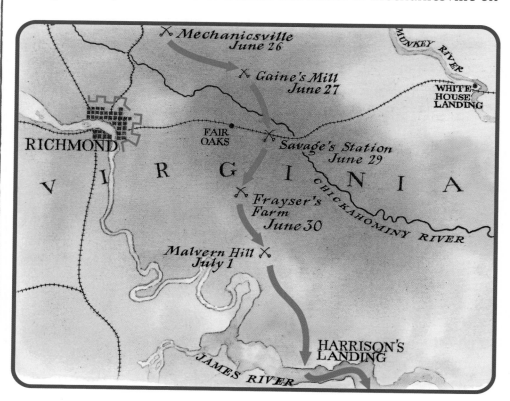

Mechanicsville
June 26

Gaine's Mill
June 27

MUNKEY RIVER

WHITE HOUSE LANDING

RICHMOND

FAIR OAKS

Savage's Station
June 29

VIRGINIA

CHICKAHOMINY RIVER

Frayser's Farm
June 30

Malvern Hill
July 1

HARRISON'S LANDING

JAMES RIVER

June 26 was the first of the so-called Seven Days' Campaign. Union forces were pushed back and eventually forced to withdraw south of the river.

Pressed by Lee, McClellan gave up any idea of attacking Richmond. In the rest of the battles of the Seven Days' Campaign, he had to fight to avoid a knock-out blow from Lee. By July 2, McClellan's army was back at the James River: his Peninsular Campaign had failed.

ASK YOURSELF

Robert E. Lee is usually seen as the best commander of the war. What might have happened if Johnston's injury had not allowed Lee to take command?

THE RIGHT ANSWER

?

Could the Peninsular Campaign have succeeded with a different Union commander?

McClellan had the vision to plan the campaign, but most historians now think that his character was the major reason it failed. Each time his Army of the Potomac should have attacked the enemy, McClellan hesitated. The siege of Yorktown was a mistake. He also split his army on either side of the Chickahominy River. There were few bridges, so the two sides could not communicate. McClellan also underestimated how many men he needed to protect his supply base at Mechanicsville. It was easy for Lee's men to attack there and at Gaines' Mill, forcing a retreat.

Chancellorsville

The Battle of Chancellorsville was fought on May 1–4, 1863. It was one of the clearest examples in the war of the tactical brilliance of the Confederate commander, Robert E. Lee.

U nion forces had failed to take Fredericksburg, Virginia, in December 1862. The Army of the Potomac and the Confederate Army of Northern Virginia spent winter facing one another across the Rappahannock River.

🔊 *A painting of the accidental shooting of the Confederate hero "Stonewall" Jackson.*

A new plan

The Army of the Potomac had a new commander, Joseph "Fighting Joe" Hooker. He was famous for being aggressive. Hooker divided his army and took half of it—75,000 men—upstream to attack Lee's Army of Northern Virginia from behind. The remaining 40,000 men stayed at Fredericksburg.

By April 30, Hooker's troops had crossed the river into an area of dense woodland known as the Wilderness. The center of their position was a crossroads at Chancellorsville. When Lee realized where the Union army was, he attacked. Like Hooker, Lee divided his forces. He marched

COMMENT

Dividing troops into smaller units was usually considered a risky tactic.

50,000 men west to meet Hooker, leaving 10,000 men in Fredericksburg under Jubal A. Early.

At noon on May 1, Lee attacked Hooker's lead divisions. Taken completely by surprise, Hooker lost his nerve. By mid-afternoon, he had stopped the advance. He ordered his forces back to Chancellorsville to defend themselves.

Jackson's surprise march

Now Lee could lead the action. He divided his army again on May 2. In one of the boldest moves of the war, he sent Thomas J. "Stonewall" Jackson and 28,000 men on a 12-mile (19 km) march to attack Hooker's right flank. That left his remaining troops to face three Union corps.

Jackson's men marched all day. At 6:00 P.M., they attacked the Union XI Corps, which promptly fled. It was only nightfall that saved

Communications at the time of the war were generally poor. A number of times, commanders were taken completely by surprise when the enemy appeared.

⤵ *The Union right wing uses a ford to cross the Rappahannock River on their way into battle.*

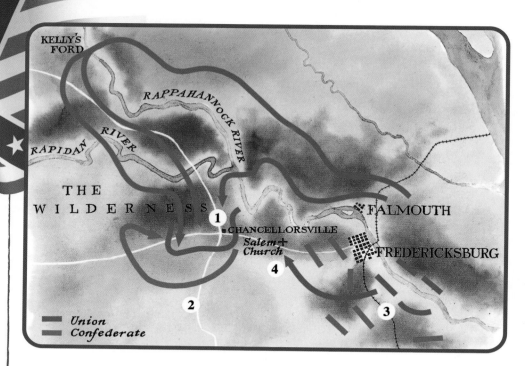

KELLY'S
FORD

RAPPAHANNOCK RIVER

RAPIDAN RIVER

THE
WILDERNESS

1

CHANCELLORSVILLE

Salem +
Church

4

FALMOUTH

FREDERICKSBURG

2

3

— Union
— Confederate

⌂ **This map shows the main positions in Fredericksburg and around Chancellorsville. Jackson's march (2) was decisive in the campaign.**

Hooker's army. The same evening, however, Jackson was accidentally shot by his own men as he returned from a patrol. They mistook his party for Union cavalry. Jackson was fatally injured.

J.E.B. Stuart took charge of Jackson's brigade. On May 3, he attacked again, while Lee attacked from the south. Together, they forced the Union line north from Chancellorsville toward the river. When a shell exploded near to Hooker, the shocked Union general handed command to Darius Couch.

Narrow escape

The Union was on the verge of a complete defeat. But meanwhile, the remaining Union troops at Fredericksburg had managed to overcome Early's

Hooker had begun the battle with a positive reputation. His defeat by Lee destroyed his confidence, and he gave up command.

troops. The Union commander, John Sedgwick, was now able to head west to help the retreating Hooker. On May 4, Lee attacked Sedgwick and stopped his advance at Salem Church.

On the night of May 5, Hooker and his men withdrew across the Rappahannock River. The Union army had been defeated by an army half its size. Casualties were high, totalling more than 17,000. The Confederate casualties alone were 12,800. They included the irreplaceable Jackson, who died a few days later from his injuries.

🎧 *This drawing shows the Union withdrawal toward the Rappahannock.*

THE RIGHT ANSWER

?

Was the Battle of Chancellorsville worth fighting from a Confederate point of view?

The high number of casualties made the battle very expensive for the Confederates. In particular, the loss of "Stonewall" Jackson was a major blow that damaged morale throughout the South. But despite the casualties, the battle was a triumph for Lee. Outnumbered two to one, he used bold tactics that brought him a resounding victory. He proved himself far more able than his counterpart, Joseph Hooker. President Lincoln's annoyance with Hooker later led him to accept Hooker's resignation. The Army of the Potomac again needed a new commander.

Siege of Vicksburg

Union general Ulysses S. Grant fought to take Vicksburg, Mississippi, from December 1862 to July 1863. If he could capture the city, the Union would control the whole Mississippi River.

The fortress city of Vicksburg sits high above a loop in the Mississippi. It dominated trade in a huge area between New Orleans and Memphis. By June 1862, both those cities were under Union control. Vicksburg was now the only city linking the two halves of the Confederacy together. If the Union could take Vicksburg, the Confederacy would be split in two. Confederate president Jefferson Davis ordered it to be held at all costs.

Grant planned his first assault on Vicksburg in December 1862. It had to be abandoned after Confederate raiders destroyed Grant's main supply base at Holly Springs, Mississippi, on December 20.

Because the Mississippi River protected the city to the west, Grant now planned to attack from the

⟳ **Union soldiers in their trenches overlooking the Mississippi River during the siege.**

Union soldiers attack an enemy position during the Siege of Vicksburg.

east. He decided to move his army through the flooded lowland swamps out of sight of the Confederate guns, cross the river, and then attack from the high ground. During the winter, he tried three times to cross the river. All attempts failed.

Throughout the war, control of the rivers was key. The Union's riverboat fleet gave it an advantage.

A new tactic

At the end of March, Grant came up with a new plan. This time, the army cut its way through the swamps to reach the Mississippi about 30 miles (48 km) to the south. Meanwhile, Union gunboats commanded by David D. Porter sailed past Vicksburg at night, avoiding the city's guns. On April 30, the gunboats carried the Union forces across the river, while William T. Sherman attacked north of the city as a diversion.

Once he had crossed the river, Grant marched east. He wanted to keep the Confederate army in Vicksburg apart from another under Joseph E.

Johnston, at Jackson, Mississippi.

Grant's army clashed with Johnston's army on May 14 and forced it back to Jackson. Grant then turned to face General John C. Pemberton, who had led his army out from Vicksburg. On May 16 and 17, Grant defeated Pemberton twice in succession, at Champion's Hill and then at Big Black River. Pemberton retreated into Vicksburg on May 18. After two failed assaults, Grant decided to lay siege to the city.

⟳ This map details the route Grant took when he successfully made it to Vicksburg after several failed attempts.

Besieged!

The Union army dug 15 miles (24 km) of trenches around Vicksburg. They brought up 220 heavy

guns to attack the city day and night. Inside the city, civilians suffered as badly as the soldiers. Many hid in caves in hillsides behind the city. Food soon ran out, and by late June, only mule and rat meat was left.

↻ *Union attackers and Confederate defenders hurl hand grenades at each other during the Siege of Vicksburg.*

Pemberton was low on ammunition. There was no hope of being relieved. He tried to negotiate a surrender with Grant, but Grant would only accept unconditional surrender. On July 4, 1863, Pemberton finally surrendered, and Grant's troops entered the city.

THE RIGHT ANSWER

?

How important was the capture of Vicksburg to the outcome of the Civil War?

The capture of Vicksburg was a huge morale boost for the Union and a massive blow for the Confederates. Grant had needed all his tactical skill and imagination to devise a route to get his troops in a position to assault the city. The Confederate leaders, on the other hand, were lulled into a false sense of security by the city's strategic defenses. Confederate president Jefferson Davis had ordered Vicksburg to be held at all costs. With the fall of the city, the Confederacy was split into two. It would never become whole again.

Gettysburg

The largest battle of the Civil War lasted for three days, from July 1–3, 1863. General Robert E. Lee's Confederate Army of Northern Virginia fought the Union Army of the Potomac of George G. Meade.

🎧 **This drawing shows the second day of Gettysburg, July 2, 1863.**

With Vicksburg under siege, Robert E. Lee wanted to begin a Confederate offensive. He ordered 75,000 men of the Army of Northern Virginia across the Potomac to invade the North on June 16, 1863.

On July 1, a Confederate unit was looking for supplies near Gettysburg, Pennsylvania, when it unexpectedly met a brigade from the Union 1st Cavalry Division.

Chance meeting

Neither side had known the other was in the area. Once Lee and the Union commander George G. Meade learned of the skirmish at Gettysburg, they both sent more troops to the town. A battle quickly became inevitable.

Fighting started on the afternoon of July 1 to the north of the town. The Confederates pushed back the Union XI Corps through the streets. The Union forces were on the verge of defeat, but they were saved by the arrival of Winfield Scott Hancock and his II Corps. At the close of the first day, the Confederates held Gettysburg, but Union forces were secure on Cemetery Hill and Culp's Hill, a little to the east. Both armies took the opportunity to reinforce during the night.

The town of Gettysburg lay at a strategically important point where roads from Washington, Baltimore, and Harrisburg met.

The next day

At dawn on July 2, Meade's 90,000 men were arranged on the high ground in a shape like a fishhook. The line ran from Culp's Hill around Cemetery Hill and south along Cemetery Ridge. On the Confederate side, Lee ordered three corps to take position along Seminary Ridge.

Fighting began that afternoon. At once, disaster struck the Union. Daniel E. Sickles led III Corps forward from Cemetery Ridge without orders. III Corps was destroyed in brutal fighting around the Peach Orchard and Devil's Den. The

This painting of Confederate infantry shows Pickett's Charge on the last day of the battle.

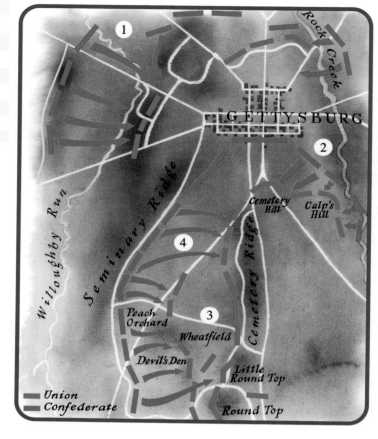

➲ **This map shows the different positions of the two sides. The Union's stronger position on the ridge left the Confederates exposed on the lower slopes.**

By the end of the second day, the Union troops were in a stronger defensive position than the Confederates.

Union left flank was also now exposed. But just in time, Union troops occupied Little Round Top, a hill that overlooked the whole battle line, and fought off Confederate attempts to capture it. Confederate attacks on Cemetery Hill and Culp's Hill also failed. Meade still held his ground.

The final day

On July 3, Lee made a decisive bid to break the Union center on Cemetery Ridge. At 1:00 P.M., 150 guns started the biggest Confederate artillery bombardment of the war. It lasted for two hours.

Around 3:00 P.M., the guns stopped. Now George E. Pickett led what became known as "Pickett's Charge." The 15,000 infantry marched steadily over a mile of open ground toward the well-defended Union position. They came under ceaseless artillery and rifle fire. Only a handful of men made it to the Union line.

Lee had made a massive tactical error. On July 4, he ordered his defeated army back to Virginia. He had suffered 20,000 casualties; the Union total was 23,000. More than 6,000 dead from both sides remained on the battlefield.

After Gettysburg, the Confederacy never again threatened the Union capital.

> Lee thought he could win the battle through sheer numbers, but he was wrong.

ASK YOURSELF

After the battle, famous photographs of dead soldiers appeared in the press. What effect might they have had on public opinion?

THE RIGHT ANSWER

?

Why is Gettysburg so often seen as a turning point in the course of the war?

Confederate General Robert E. Lee knew that to have any chance of winning the war, he had to take Washington, D.C. He was advancing there when the battle unexpectedly started at Gettysburg. Lee's commanders were outwitted by their Union counterparts. But the biggest failure was Lee's. His decision to send Pickett's troops across 1 mile (1.6 km) of open ground was madness. Union troops behind stone walls fired freely into the advancing enemy. Pickett's Charge, as it became known, marked not just the end of the battle, but of Confederate hopes of overall victory.

Siege of Petersburg

Between June 1864 and March 1865, General Ulysses S. Grant's Union Army of the Potomac lay siege to General Robert E. Lee's Confederate Army of Northern Virginia at Petersburg, Virginia.

COMMENT

Petersburg was an important railroad center. Two lines into and out of Richmond went through the town.

◔ **Union troops appear on the defenses during the fall of Petersburg.**

As early as July 1862, it was clear that the Confederate capital at Richmond, Virginia, could be attacked from the south. Petersburg guarded the southern approach to the city. It was an obvious strategic target for the Union.

The Union's first advance on Richmond, in summer 1862, had failed. On June 15, 1864, Grant decided to try to attack the city again from the river. He ordered the 100,000-strong Army of the Potomac to travel south from Cold Harbor and west through Petersburg. They would attack the Army of Northern Virginia, which was defending Richmond, from the rear.

Lines are drawn

A Confederate force hastily organized by General P. G. T. Beauregard stopped the Union advance at Petersburg. Two days later, Lee ordered most of his army to move south to

protect the city and its railroad. His men set up lines of defenses southeast of the city that could withstand any frontal assault. But Grant had foreseen that. He kept his army to the west and the south. His main goal was to capture the two railroads that led to Petersburg, which were used to supply Lee's army. His other target was the Appomattox River, which was Lee's line of retreat to the west.

Union troops huddle in their trenches during the Siege of Petersburg as they await their next order.

The Confederates suffer

The two sides fought several battles. When the Union won no advantage, Grant ordered trenches to be dug around the city. The siege had begun.

In late August, Union forces succeeded in cutting the railroad running south. Grant attacked again in late September and late October. He also extended the siege lines to 35 miles (56 km). They eventually stretched from

The city of Petersburg lies on the south side of the Appomattox River, 23 miles (37 km) south of Richmond.

the eastern edge of Richmond to the south and east of Petersburg. As the trench lines grew longer, the last rail line open to Lee came under threat. Lee's position was now desperate. Confederate stores were falling rapidly, and new supplies could no longer get through. Lee was now heavily outnumbered. He did not have enough troops to man all the fortifications.

The situation worsens

During the winter, the siege degenerated into a grim form of trench warfare. Soldiers on both sides suffered from the harsh conditions. This stalemate continued until February 1865, when Grant renewed his attacks.

On March 29, Grant began a final push. He sent 125,000 men to outflank Lee's trench line. At the Battle of Five Forks on April 1, they overwhelmed

⟳ **This battery of Union 20-pound guns was set up in the trenches around Petersburg.**

an enemy force of 10,000. The Confederates lost around one-third of their men, compared with Union casualties of just 800. More importantly, Lee's last escape route was closed off.

Lee withdraws

Lee realized that he could no longer withstand the Union assault. On the evening of April 2, the Confederate withdrawal from Petersburg began. The next day, at 9 A.M., Grant and his Union troops entered the city. Lee meanwhile retreated west to try to join forces with General Joseph E. Johnston in North Carolina. That plan failed—and the defeat of the Confederacy was imminent.

ASK YOURSELF

Why did it matter whether or not Lee had an escape route for his army? Couldn't he keep fighting anyway?

THE RIGHT ANSWER

?

Was the outcome of the Siege of Petersburg inevitable from the start?

Simply because of the numbers involved, the siege was always weighted in favor of the Union. Union troops numbered as many as 125,000, while the Confederate force was never more than around 50,000. At the end of the siege, casualties stood at 42,000 Union and 28,000 Confederate soldiers—but the Union besiegers could afford to lose more men than the besieged defenders. As desertion rates rose and casualties increased during the 10-month siege, the number of men available to Lee fell even more dramatically. Ultimately, a Union victory was assured.

March to the Sea

In late 1864, Union general William T. Sherman led his troops through Georgia and the Carolinas. The soldiers destroyed everything in their path in a show of strength intended to terrify Southerners.

⌃ **Union soldiers destroy railroad tracks during the March to the Sea.**

COMMENT

Sherman believed in "total war." He said he wanted everyone in the South to feel "the hard hand of war."

Sherman captured Atlanta, Georgia, in September 1864. His supply lines were still being attacked, however. Unable to protect his lines, Sherman decided to move somewhere that could be supplied by sea. He decided to march to Savannah, Georgia, 220 miles (352 km) away.

The march had two aims. First, Sherman needed to secure supplies for his army. Second, he wanted to break Southern spirit by making civilians suffer. He said that on their march his troops would "smash things generally."

March of destruction

Sherman set fire to anything in Atlanta that might have a military use. Then he led his 60,000 men southeast toward Savannah.They met no resistance. The Confederate Army of Tennessee had seized the chance to launch an invasion of Tennessee; the invasion eventually failed.

As the Union troops advanced, they wrecked anything that might help the Confederate war effort, such as factories and railroad lines. Troops often behaved badly. They stole and vandalized. They treated Southerners they met badly. Some

With no opposition, Sherman spread his army across an area up to 60 miles (96 km) wide. This made it easier to find enough food.

RAILROAD DEPOT AT RESACA, GEORGIA.

ADAIRSVILLE, GEORGIA.

KINGSTON, GEORGIA.

WOODLANDS, GEORGIA.

☞ *Etchings published in the Harper's Weekly magazine in 1864 show events from Sherman's March to the Sea through Georgia.*

of the worst treated were the African American slaves freed by the Union army.

Sherman captured Savannah on December 21, 1864. He then joined Ulysses S. Grant in Virginia to defeat Robert E. Lee's army on the Richmond–Petersburg front. Sherman then decided on a second march through the Carolinas.

March through the Carolinas

The march began on February 1, 1865. It was much harder than the first. Confederate troops were waiting, and the terrain was much more difficult. Sherman's route lay along muddy roads and swampy rivers. But Confederate leaders were surprised by the speed of the Union advance.

They were also horrified by the brutality of Sherman's men. The destruction was much worse

↻ *Union troops marched 600 miles (960 km) through Georgia and the Carolinas.*

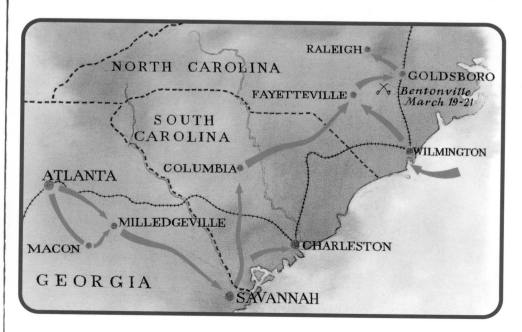

than in Georgia. One reason was that many Union soldiers blamed South Carolina for causing the war, because it had been the first state to secede. They took their revenge by burning towns and homes.

Joseph E. Johnston's Confederates failed to stop the Union progress at Bentonville in March. Sherman occupied Raleigh, the state capital, a few days later. Within weeks, the war was over. Johnston surrendered to Sherman on April 26. Sherman's marches had proved decisive.

⊙ *This engraving shows freedmen following the Union army during the March to the Sea in late 1864.*

ASK YOURSELF

Would the war have lasted longer without Sherman's march? Or, was the South already all but defeated?

THE RIGHT ANSWER

?

Was the level of destruction carried out by Sherman's troops really necessary?

Sherman believed that a massive show of strength would destroy the morale of Southern civilians. He understood that psychological suffering could be just as important as physical suffering. This is the concept of "total war." By taking the war to civilians, ordinary people would see that there was no means of escape. To that extent, the destruction was necessary. However, it proved impossible to control the thousands of lawless stragglers who followed the Union army. They carried out atrocities that appalled even Sherman's battle-hardened generals.

Road to Appomattox

The last major campaign of the Civil War saw the final defeat of Robert E. Lee's Confederate Army of Northern Virginia. On April 9, 1865, Lee surrendered to Union general Ulysses S. Grant.

COMMENT

By spring, Lee knew that his Army of Northern Virginia faced certain defeat, but he would not give up.

⟳ *A Union charge routs the enemy during the Battle of Five Forks.*

By spring 1865, Union armies dominated the eastern theater of the war. William T. Sherman's march through the South had devastated Georgia and the Carolinas. His only remaining opposition was Joseph E. Johnston's much-reduced Army of Tennessee. In Virginia, Union forces under Ulysses S. Grant had captured Petersburg following a 10-month siege. The Confederate situation was desperate.

The fight continues

Lee wanted to continue the fight in the West by joining up with Johnston at Danville. But his exhausted men were short of stores. They hoped to receive new supplies via the Richmond and Danville Railroad. But Union troops harassed the Confederates around Amelia Court House and Tabernacle Creek and pushed them away from the railroad.

Wilmer McLean's house in Appomattox Court House, where Lee surrendered the Army of Northern Virginia to Grant.

Meanwhile, Union cavalry blocked Lee's route south. Lee was forced to set out westward, but Union forces were catching up. Lee led his men on a rapid night march west to Rice's Station on the Southside Railroad. Many starving and sick soldiers dropped out during the night, too exhausted to continue.

Battle of Sayler's Creek

Union troops attacked the Confederate rear guard near Sayler's Creek on April 6. Both sides suffered heavy losses, but the effects of the losses were worse for the Confederates.

In one encounter, a small Union force—about 600 infantry and cavalry—was cut off at High Bridge, which carried the Southside Railroad over the Appomattox River. The Union force had hoped to destroy the bridge to prevent Lee from crossing, but they failed. The officers in charge,

The Battle of Sayler's Creek resulted in the loss of one-third of Lee's army—between 7,000 and 8,000 men, including six generals.

⟲ *After evacuating Petersburg and Richmond, Lee's exhausted Confederates struggled west to meet with Johnston's army.*

Theodore Read and Francis Washburn, decided to sacrifice their command to delay Lee. They repeatedly charged the advancing Confederate columns. Both the commanders and many of their men died in the attempt.

On April 7, Lee led his men across the Appomattox in an attempt to reach Lynchburg. Union troops were not far behind. Confederate supplies had finally reached Appomattox Station, but Union cavalry got there first and seized them. Lee was now trapped between three Union forces. He sent 1,600 infantry and 2,400 cavalry to try to force a breakout, but they made little headway.

The end arrives

Some of Lee's junior officers tried to persuade him to scatter his army. They wanted to continue the war in small bands of guerrillas. But Lee could see that, even if two-thirds of his remaining 15,000 troops escaped—which was unlikely—

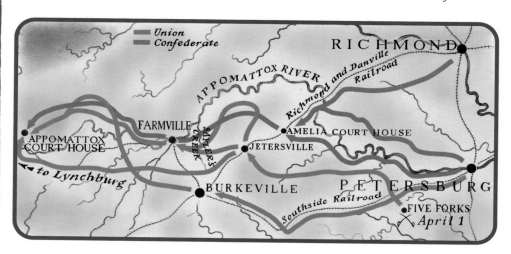

there were not enough of them to be effective. He had no other choice but to surrender. He said: "There is nothing left for me to do but to go and see General Grant, and I would rather die a thousand deaths."

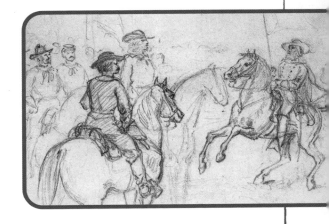

April 9, 1865, happened to be Palm Sunday. At 1.00 P.M., General Robert E. Lee rode to the small settlement of Appomattox Court House. There, he surrendered the main army of the Confederacy to General Ulysses S. Grant of the Union. The end of the war had come.

In this drawing, Union general George Custer (center) accepts a flag of truce from a Confederate officer.

THE RIGHT ANSWER

?

What was the significance of Lee's surrender of the Army of Northern Virginia?

The Army of Northern Virginia was the greatest army of the Confederacy. Other Confederate forces remained in the field, and some officers wanted to fight on. Without Lee's army, however, they would have been unable to resist the Union forces. Over the next few weeks, they all surrendered. Without armed forces to protect it, the Confederate government was powerless. President Jefferson Davis fled after the fall of the Confederate capital, Richmond. He held a cabinet meeting on May 5, 1865, in Georgia and dissolved the government. The Confederacy was at an end.

Glossary

artillery: Heavy guns such as cannons and mortars that are used to attack enemy defenses.

battery: A group of heavy guns or artillery pieces.

blockade: A system of ships that intercept vessels in order to prevent a country or other body from being able to trade.

bombardment: A sustained artillery attack on a target.

brigade: A military unit that has about 5,000 soldiers, divided into up to six regiments.

cavalry: Part of the army that fights on horseback.

Confederacy: The word used to describe the Southern side in the Civil War.

counterattack: To launch an attack on the enemy as a response to an enemy attack.

flank: The side of a military unit or position.

fortifications: Strong defenses, such as walls or trenches.

infantry: Soldiers who are trained to fight on foot.

ironclad: A warship that has a protective covering of iron armor.

morale: The mental and emotional condition of an individual or group.

regiment: A military unit; at full strength, a Civil War regiment had 10 companies of 100 men each.

rout: To defeat totally.

siege: An attack that cuts off a military position or city to force it to surrender.

skirmish: A minor fight between small numbers of soldiers.

strategic: A word that describes something that is important to achieving an overall goal, even if it may not be very important on its own.

tactics: The science and art of maneuvering forces in combat.

Further reading

Abnett, Dan. **Gamble for Victory: Battle of Gettysburg** (Graphic History). Osprey Publishing, 2006.

Beller, Susan Provost. **Billy Yank and Johnny Reb: Soldiering in the Civil War.** Twenty-First Century Books, 2007.

Burgan, Michael. **The Battle of Gettysburg** (Graphic Library, Graphic History). Capstone Press, 2006.

Cohn, Scotti. **Beyond Their Years: Stories of Sixteen Civil War Children.** TwoDot, 2003.

Hama, Larry. **Surprise Attack! The Battle of Shiloh** (Graphic History). Osprey Publishing, 2006.

Hama, Larry. **The War Is On! Battle of First Bull Run** (Graphic History). Osprey Publishing, 2007.

Rice, Earle. **Robert E. Lee: First Soldier of the Confederacy** (Civil War Leaders). Morgan Reynolds Publishing, 2005.

Stanchak, John E. **Eyewitness Civil War.** Dorling Kindersley, 2011.

Warren, Andrea. **Under Siege! Three Children at the Civil War Battle for Vicksburg.** Melanie Kroupa Books, 2009.

Websites

History Place interactive timeline of the Civil War.
http//www.historyplace.com/civilwar

Smithsonian Institution page with resources on the Civil War.
http//www.civilwar.si.edu

ThinkQuest site for students that divides battles into Union victories, Confederate victories, and indecisive battles.
http://library.thinkquest.org/3055/netscape/battles/

A site supporting the PBS film *The Civil War*, directed by Ken Burns.
http//www.pbs.org/civilwar

Publisher's note to educators and parents: Our editors have carefully reviewed these websites to ensure that they are suitable for students. Many websites change frequently, however, and we cannot guarantee that a site's future contents will continue to meet our high standards of quality and educational value. Be advised that students should be closely supervised whenever they access the Internet.

Index